Copyright © 2014 by Butta 'Fly' Jonez
All rights reserved. This book or any portion thereof
may not be reproduced or used in any manner whatsoever
without the express written permission of the publisher
except for the use of brief quotations in a book review.

Printed in the United States of America

First Printing, 2014

ISBN: **978-1500885885**

Street Queen Media
P.O. Box 60040
Chicago, Illinois 60660

Website: ButtaJonez.com

Email Address: streetqueenmedia@gmail.com

INTRODUCTION

My name is Butta 'Fly' Jonez. I am a dating strategist and seduction expert. You may know me from the blog PeepGame.Net – *The World's First Playa's Guide for Women*. Or, you may know me from my first book, "How to be a Female Player".

I teach women the GAME of DATING – how to date strategically and consciously – how to create relationships with the men they want and truly deserve. I have spent close to 15 years mastering my craft and at this point I am truly a master of THE GAME.

It is now my mission to teach other women how to play the game of love effectively.

I spent the last year developing a series of books that will teach women all of my strategies, all of my techniques, all of my tricks for attracting, seducing, gaming and taming men. From the fundamentals of mackin' to getting money from men, attracting men in droves to seducing men, juggling a stable of men to getting a ring in 365. My books will teach YOU how to date strategically and effectively…like a female player.

Let me take a moment to define that term. A female player is a woman who understands how men think. She's a woman who knows how to gain and keep the leverage in relationships. She dates for benefit…for gain of some kind. A female player knows how to get the men she dates to give her what she wants without giving much (if anything) in return. That in short, is a female player.

I am a female player and I can turn you into one…TODAY!

I can help you transform your dating life so that it is more enjoyable than ever before. I can teach you how to spot the kind of men who will give you what you want and I can teach you how to avoid the men who will waste your time. I can teach you how to get money from the men you date without having sex with them. I can tell you how to go from 'friend' to fiancé in less than a year. I can tell you how to set the pace of a relationship…and so much more.

But today, I am going to teach you one thing--how to attract wealthy men and develop lasting relationships with them!

I've coached hundreds of women over the last 5 years and I discovered through these sessions that many women want to date men above their economic level. In essence they want to date UP. And I wasn't surprised by that fact. After all, it is basically instinctual for women to desire the strongest, most powerful, most capable man in a social circle. A man who can provide comfort is highly desirable in any group, and that has been the case since the caveman times.

That being said, you are not alone! Your desire to meet, date and marry a rich man is not only normal, it is natural.

What I am going to show you today is HOW you can accomplish your goal, how you can date rich and marry well. I am going to give you a workable plan that will help you attract rich men into your life, and help you establish lasting relationships with them.

I have shared these same tips with my clients and have witnessed them go on to meet celebrities and wealthy men, and to develop lasting relationships with them. These women are just like you. They started out just like you.

Now, I am going to give you what has already been given to them.

And, you will succeed IF you work my *Date Rich, Marry Well* plan.

You see, success in any THING requires focus, practice and patience. If you apply those three things to any good thing, you will most certainly achieve success. That said, really focus on the strategies in this workbook and practice them with patience so that you achieve the results you desire.

There are millions of wealthy men around the world, at least one million in the United States alone. You can have one of them…you should have one of them. In fact, you can start meeting and dating wealthy men today IF you utilize the methods in this book.

I have the techniques you need to succeed. I am giving you what you need to win. All you have to do is believe in yourself, follow my advice and take action.

Are you ready to take your dating game to the next level Playa? Well let's waste no time…PEEP GAME!

Step 1

REMOVE JUDGMENT

Deciding to date men with means is a personal choice and a viable option for most women. However, making that decision – to date rich - will often bring up thoughts and beliefs that are in conflict with your decision.

For example:

- **Women who date men FOR MONEY are gold-diggers**

- **Women who seek out rich men have NOTHING going for themselves**

- **Women who date wealthy men are LOOSE--merely exchanging sex for money and/or gifts**

These thoughts and beliefs surely can be validated by women we see in the media and women we know personally. The world view is that women who date rich men exclusively or predominately are conniving tricksters incapable of loving anything but the money in a man's pocket.

Most women shudder at the thought of being viewed as LOOSE, CONNIVING or a GOLD DIGGER, so rather than pursue their desired relationship, they settle for what is readily available and widely acceptable.

If you want to ATTRACT wealthy men into your life, you are going to have to FIRST release the judgments you have about WOMEN WHO DATE MEN FOR MONEY.

Here's how you do that!

-DECIDE WHO YOU ARE AND WHAT YOU REALLY WANT-

Telling the truth about a situation helps release the judgments you are holding about that situation. This is the first step in creation. You see, judgments are nothing more than widely accepted social norms.

- **Love is better than money -> MONEY SHOULD NOT BE A FACTOR WHEN YOU'RE LOOKING FOR A GOOD MAN!**
- **Money is the root of all evil -> MARRY FOR LOVE OR FOR THE MONEY! YOU WON'T GET BOTH IN ONE MAN.**
- **A strong woman doesn't need a man -> IF YOU EDUCATE YOURSELF AND PURSUE YOUR PROFESSIONAL GOALS, YOU WON'T NEED A MAN TO TAKE CARE OF YOU!**
- **An independent woman doesn't need a man's money -> REAL WOMEN TAKE CARE OF THEMSELVES (FINANCIALLY)!**

These are what I call *The World View*. These limited beliefs are the reason why many women settle for men who have little or nothing to offer financially. Instead of pursuing their unique relationship goals, they rationalize why it's better to date the men who are readily available rather than pursue the kind of man they truly desire.

Few women step outside the box and GO FOR THE GOLD! I believe that's because they don't know how to create the relationship of their dreams. They don't know how to define, visualize and manifest A LOVING, NURTURING, SUPPORTIVE, PROTECTIVE…**RICH MAN.**

If, however, you want to create a new relationship reality, you must first identify and define that relationship. You must uncover your personal truth.

Your personal truth is the voice inside that is telling YOU what YOU really want.

It is telling you, I want to live luxuriously. It is telling you, I want a rich partner who can provide unlimited comfort. It is telling you, I want to live in a mansion and drive a luxury car. It is telling you I want to date rich and marry well.

That voice is a guide. It is screaming, "This is my truth!" *Will you listen?*

Haven't you heard? The truth will set you free! Yes it will.

When you acknowledge and validate your personal truth, those judgments that have kept you from pursuing, dating or even considering wealthy men will fall by the wayside.

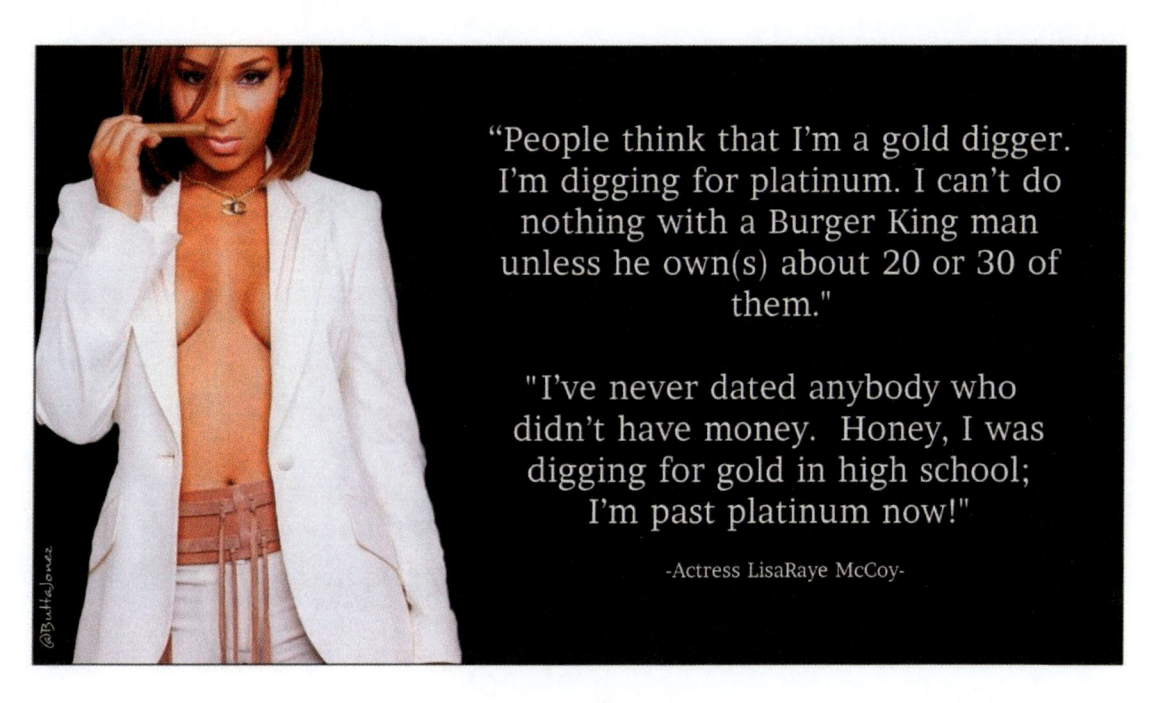

"People think that I'm a gold digger. I'm digging for platinum. I can't do nothing with a Burger King man unless he own(s) about 20 or 30 of them."

"I've never dated anybody who didn't have money. Honey, I was digging for gold in high school; I'm past platinum now!"

-Actress LisaRaye McCoy-

Actress LisaRaye States Her 'Truth'

When it comes to dating men with money, what is your personal truth? Take a minute to write that out.

MY TRUTH IS…

_____
_____
_____
_____
_____
_____
_____

You have just written your truth statement about dating rich men. That is the first step to creating your new relationship reality. Congratulations!

Let's move on to another very important point.

-EVERY CHOICE COMES WITH A UNIQUE SET OF CIRCUMSTANCES-

You've just made a choice – to *Date Rich and Marry Well*. That decision could literally change your life. Let's focus on that a moment so that we can really tap into and unearth your desires.

- **What are the benefits to dating men with money as you see them?**
- **How do you anticipate your life and lifestyle being transformed by dating rich and marrying well?**

Write down your ideas below:

(Examples: Frequent travel, expensive gifts, increased resources, an economically powerful social network)

1. _____
2. _____
3. _____
4. _____
5. _____
6. _____
7. _____
8. _____

This list will help you clarify your purpose for pursuing men with money. There is a WHY behind everything. You have just uncovered your **WHY**…I WANT TO DATE RICH & MARRY WELL.

Your new relationship goal has just been defined!

Step 2
UNDERSTAND THE NATURE OF MEN

Although women today are capable of earning just as much as or more than a man, it is NATURAL FOR MAN to provide FOR HIS WOMAN.

There is a sense of pride that men feel when they can supply what their woman needs. She may have money of her own, but HIS PRIDE comes from what HE brings to the table.

MEN ARE HUNTERS!
EVEN IN 2014 MEN LIKE TO BRING HOME THE BACON

Sure things have changed since the olden days.

We no longer live in caves.

Divorce is an option.

Women today are breadwinners.

But some things don't change with time. One of those things is man's nature.

Despite a lot of the rhetoric spewed in media, you will find most men want to give THEIR CHOSEN WOMAN comfort; they want to make her way easy and her burden light so to speak. These are his instincts. And many women, despite being breadwinners in their own right, appreciate dating or being married to a man who has resources.

POWER COUPLE
WHEN TWO FINANCIALLY EQUITABLE PEOPLE COME TOGETHER IN A ROMANTIC PARTNERSHIP

It doesn't matter what his woman has or can do for herself. A man's inner drive is to satisfy his lady's needs. If a man has resources, it is natural for him to provide.

And that goes for wealthy men as well. Rich men enjoy bringing home the bacon. Some say their drive to provide is even higher than the average guy. In fact, a rich man has enough money to spoil his woman...not just meet her needs. That's a whole different level of comfort. He can afford to splurge on his woman, to give her everything she wants, needs and desires.

And that right there, is why rich men are so sought after by women even in 2014. The rich man provides on a level that is virtually limitless. Dating him is like being a kid in a candy store. You can have almost anything you desire. Exotic vacations, exquisite diamonds, 5-Star dinners? That's life with a rich man. He is ready, willing and able to spoil and splurge.

And let me make another important point. The rich man understands THE GAME! He knows he's rich; he knows he's the alpha male in society; he knows he has what women want; AND, he knows it is expected of him to share what's in his pockets. Just like beautiful women know men pursue her because she's beautiful, wealthy men know it's their bank account (not necessarily their physical attributes) that bring the girls to the yard.

Forget what you've heard in the media! Stop feeling guilty about wanting to *Date Rich and Marry Well*. Know that you are making a conscious decision to date men who can provide for you at the level of your comfort. That is dating smart. That is dating with an end goal in mind. That is called having a game plan.

And your decision makes sense! Even rich men understand and relate to your financially conscious approach to dating. Just ask multi-millionaire, 50 Cent.

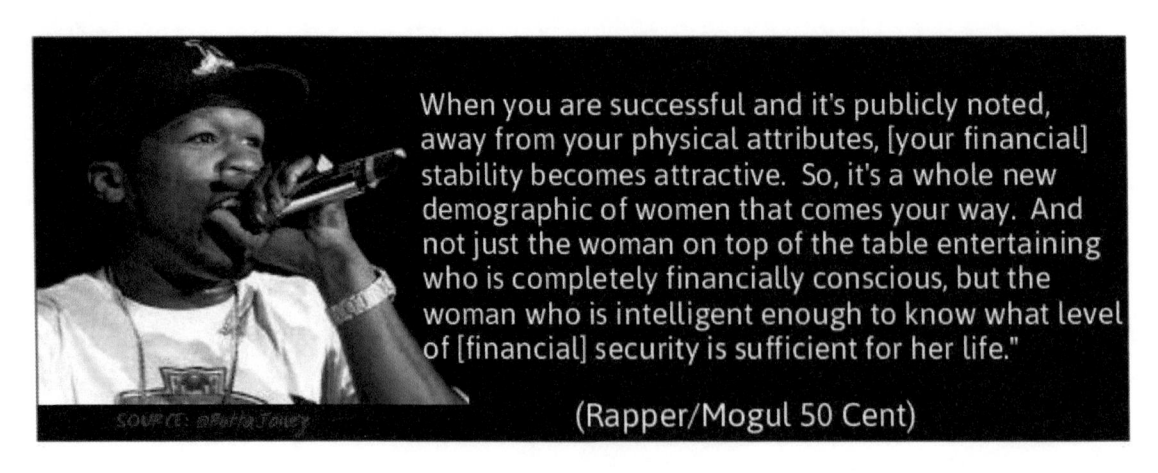

> "When you are successful and it's publicly noted, away from your physical attributes, [your financial] stability becomes attractive. So, it's a whole new demographic of women that comes your way. And not just the woman on top of the table entertaining who is completely financially conscious, but the woman who is intelligent enough to know what level of [financial] security is sufficient for her life."
>
> (Rapper/Mogul 50 Cent)

Facts are often convoluted by fiction. What is real is often lost in a haze of illusion. Such is the case when it comes to women who date wealthy men. Movies depict financially conscious women as conniving coattail riders. Popular songs chastise the so-called gold-digger. Tabloid headlines frequently report stories of rich men being doggedly pursued and manipulated by money-grubbing women. Even popular relationship experts insist dating FOR LOVE is more respectable than dating FOR MONEY.

In this way facts are convoluted by fiction. In order to release judgments around exclusively or predominantly dating rich men, you must separate the facts from fiction.

FACT: Dating men WITH money doesn't not mean dating men FOR money

FACT: Women who assess a man's financial situation before deeming him suitable are "financially conscious"

FACT: 'Good' women know what is good for them and so date men who will be good to them

FACT: Bad Girls are like Bad Boys. They seek out victims not partners. They are looking for their next 'lick' NOT a relationship. A financially conscious woman is not necessarily a "bad" girl or a coattail-riding-gold digger

FACT: Money isn't everything…but it helps!

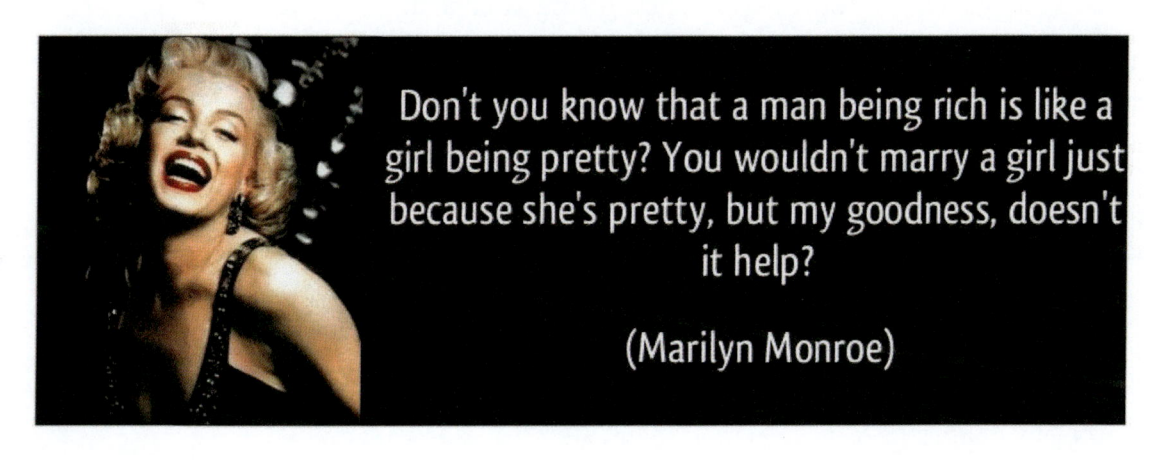

> Don't you know that a man being rich is like a girl being pretty? You wouldn't marry a girl just because she's pretty, but my goodness, doesn't it help?
>
> (Marilyn Monroe)

Step 3

FORM YOUR NEW REALITY WITH WORDS

Great is the power of our tongues! What we say inevitably becomes our reality. Our words define our world and shape our relationships. Thus it is important that what we say about men and relationships going forward…is exactly what we hope to experience going forward.

When you speak into the atmosphere words and phrases that call forth ANY 'thing', you will attract that 'thing'. This process is often referred to as The

---

**RICH MEN ARE UNCONSCIOUSLY ATTRACTED
TO WOMEN WHO WANT TO BE IN RELATIONSHIPS
WITH A RICH MAN.**

**THAT'S HOW THE TWO UNITE.
SUPPLY MEETS DEMAND OR, AS SCIENCE HAS EXPLAINED,
LIKE ATTRACTS LIKE.**

IT'S CALLED METAPHYSICS!

**THE ENERGY OF WOMEN
WHO TRULY DESIRE WEALTHY SUITORS
LITERALLY INVITES RICH MEN INTO THEIR LIVES ENERGETICALLY.**

Law of Attraction. The Law of Attraction is simply a scientific and practical way to shape reality.

If dating and/or marrying a wealthy man is what you desire, CALL FORTH that reality; then watch that experience take shape.

Let's begin!

Say this aloud:

"I now choose to date rich men and I give thanks rich men are now irresistibly attracted to me!"

When you affirm that statement --"I now choose to date rich men and I give thanks rich men are now irresistibly attracted to me," you literally energize yourself with an aura that will draw in rich men. Say that statement again right now 10 times.

You are now re-programming your mind and thus your experience with words!

I want you to begin affirming that statement daily for 5 minutes straight while looking into a mirror.

Before you begin, take several deep breaths to slow your breathing and clear your mind of extraneous thoughts.

When you finish that exercise, I want you to do one more thing. Recite my "I Attract Rich Men" meditation.

You will find this powerful meditation on the following page. This is the same meditation I used to meet and date 2 NFL players and an award winning R&B singer. It's the same meditation I gave a client who is now dating a well-known (and wealthy) actor. This is the same meditation I shared with a client who soon met and married a prominent dermatologist. This is the same meditation I also gave a model you've certainly seen in print, who is now dating multiple millionaires.

This meditation is so powerful, it shouldn't be used IF YOU ARE NOT READY OR WILLING TO DATE A RICH MAN because once you start reciting this meditation and visualizing yourself in the arms of a rich man…he will come in. Wealthy suitors will appear. They will literally be placed on your path.

One day years ago after doing this same meditation for a few days straight, I went on a modeling assignment at a television studio. While waiting in the green room for my call time an attractive man about 35 years old started talking to me. He was the nicest man and we had a great conversation about Chicago (my home town), modeling and a bunch of other stuff. I assumed the guy, like me, was in the green room waiting for his call time.

"He must be a new author" I thought. "Perhaps he's waiting for someone?" About 10 minutes into our conversation my new friend revealed who he was. He was the CEO of one of the biggest package delivery companies in the world. Not vice president, not an executive…he was THE 7-figure earning top dog of a Fortune 100 company.

As the reality of this man's position and wealth registered in my mind, the show's executive producer popped through the door and told me to get to hair and make-up ASAP. As I gathered my purse and duffle bag Mr. CEO gave me a wink and passed me his card. "You're an intelligent woman. I could use a woman like you on my corporate team. Call me."

I knew what he meant (He was letting me know to give him a call…in a professional way)

Game on!

I am not going to waste your time. I am giving you the tools you need to attract rich men into your life. I have used these tools and I have benefitted from them. Many other women have used these same tools and benefitted from them. Now it's your turn.

Take my meditation and use it. Recite it daily. Make it a part of your everyday routine. I know of no other more effective means of attracting rich men than this.

Try it now and see how your dating life transforms.

I ATTRACT RICH MEN MEDITATION

Begin to declare your desire

"I NOW CHOOSE TO DATE RICH MEN."

Declare your willingness to date rich men.

"I AM NOW WILLING TO DATE MEN WHO ARE RICH."

Declare your willingness to grow.

"I AM WILLING TO CHANGE. I AM WILLING TO GROW AND TO EXPAND. I TRUST THE PROCESS OF LIFE."

Declare rich men are now in your life.

"RICH MEN ARE IN MY LIFE RIGHT HERE AND RIGHT NOW. I AM UNITED WITH THEM NOW."

Declare the RIGHT men are now drawn to you.

"THE RIGHT MEN ARE DRAWN TO ME NOW. I AM ALWAYS IN THE RIGHT PLACE AT THE RIGHT TIME."

Affirm your worthiness.

"I AM WORTHY OF THE VERY BEST IN LIFE. I LOVINGLY ACCEPT THE VERY BEST LIFE HAS TO OFFER ME NOW."

Affirm the generosity of men.

"MEN ARE GENEROUS. THEY ALL GIVE GENEROUSLY TO ME. MEN LOVE TO SPEND MONEY ON ME. MEN LOVE TO BUY ME GIFTS."

Accept the truth.

"MEN LOVE ME AND I LOVE ALL MEN."

Picture *Mr. Rich and Wonderful* in your mind. What does he look like? Is he tall/short? Is he elegantly or casually dressed? What race is he? What is his occupation? What is his net worth?

Create the image of the rich man YOU WANT in your mind and FEEL WHAT YOU THINK IT WILL FEEL LIKE to date him.

Generate the emotions. Really try to feel what YOU THINK it will feel like to date the wealthy man you've imagined.

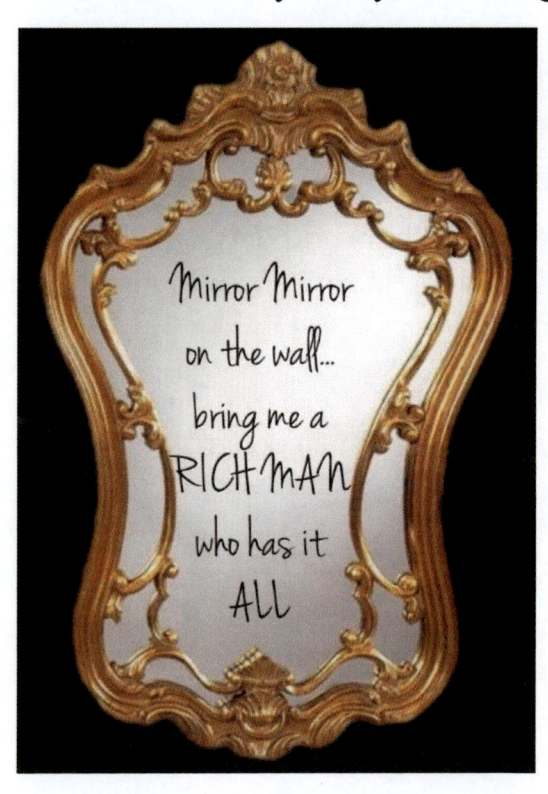

This technique is similar to the techniques used by superstar athletes to land difficult shots, to make game-winning points, and to score under pressure. It's called creative visualization. In effect, you are CREATING a future reality in your mind hours, days, minutes before it actually happens.

Masters of any sport use their mind to CREATE success. You can use similar techniques to CREATE a new relationship reality.

The best part of this creative process is the fact that once your mind accepts the statements…that you are now attractive to rich men…it accepts that reality as fact. When you achieve this state of mind, whether you recite the affirmations above daily or not, rich men will regularly come into your life.

Re-program your mind, create a whole new world!

Step 4
PUT YOURSELF IN POSITION

TAKE ACTION!

It's been said, faith without works is dead.

To truly benefit from the affirmations mentioned above, you must take some action. Hey, *Mr. Rich & Wonderful* is probably not going to show up at your door as you sit watching *Real Housewives of Beverly Hills* in your living room. Nah! The odds of that happening are slim to none.

Mr. Rich & Wonderful is in motion. He is out in the world making moves. If you want to connect with him, you will need to place yourself in his environment.

That's what women who date rich and powerful men do. They place themselves in environments where rich and powerful men congregate.

Let me give you some examples you can relate to:

1. Before becoming famous, Kim Kardashian worked as a celebrity stylist for R&B singer Brandy. Through that job, Kim connected with Brandy's brother Ray J--a well-known singer/actor in his own right. The two dated for a while before Kim moved on to bigger fish like NFL'er Reggie Bush and Rap Superstar Kanye West.

    Bottom Line: Kim put herself in a position where she could service wealthy, connected men. No pun intended. She worked the celebrity circles strategically, dating one wealthy guy after another. Eventually, Kim not only snagged a wealthy man but a multi-million dollar empire of her own as well.

The lesson? Rich men tend to date/marry the women who are in their environments. Living, working, socializing in wealthy circles is a sure way to meet potential companions.

2. I have worked for several non-profit organizations. The organizations I worked for were all supported by/promoted by wealthy donors. In one particular position, I was responsible for attracting notable business men and women as donors for a youth group. Through my job, I networked with some of the top earning professionals in the Midwest. This put me in the right position to meet wealthy bachelors. At another position at a non-profit, I shared office space with Stedman Graham, Oprah's longtime BF.

    Bottom Line: Many successful business professionals are too busy working their way up the ladder to find time to find a date. They often just approach the women who are in their environment. Working in a position that allowed me to show off my style, personality and wit worked wonders for my social calendar. The Lesson? Go where the money is! Aside from that, make sure you present yourself well and know when (or if) you should to take a professional connection to the next level.

3. I once knew a woman who lived in a beautiful apartment in a luxury building in downtown Chicago. The woman wasn't wealthy but somehow managed to get a subsidized unit in this full-amenity residence. Over time I learned that professional athletes, notable businessmen and other money-makers lived in and visited the building. This woman was literally living in the midst of wealth.

    Bottom Line: What a strategist this woman was? She didn't have to go far to find a wealthy date/mate—only step outside her front door. In the elevator, lobby, fitness room etc., rich bachelors were everywhere she looked. The lesson? Even if you don't have a lot of money, there are ways to live and/work around wealthy people. Do your research. Put your antennas up and scout out opportunities to LIVE within arm's reach of the rich and powerful.

You must go where the money is. You must insert yourself into affluent circles IF you want to meet and ultimately seduce a wealthy bachelor. I've never met a celebrity, politician or 6-figure earning business man sitting on the couch. I was always in motion and usually working/socializing in THEIR environment.

I'm going to give you a list of places you can go to increase your odds of meeting wealthy men. This list will help you narrow down the places in your city where rich, eligible bachelors can be found. When you go to the places I suggest I want you to do the following:

- **Make sure you put your best foot forward. Look your physical best.**
- **Go alone or with no more than one girlfriend who has the same agenda as you.**
- **Smile, look open and approachable.**
- **When a guy approaches you, entertain his conversation BUT excuse yourself well before you run out of things to say.**
- **Get your target guy's number and as much information as he's willing to give before you apologize and tell him you have got to go.**
- **Before leaving, suggest he call you later that evening or the very next day.**

TOP 5 PLACES TO MEET WEALTHY MEN

1. High-End Health Clubs

Many men who have a large net worth are also into physical fitness. Not just actors and athletes but younger politicians, entrepreneurs, stock brokers and bankers. These guys work a routine daily – mental, physical and social. How else does one ascend to the highest income brackets? That said, get a membership to one of the high-end health clubs in your area. Not only are you likely to meet local moguls, but visiting celebrities, athletes and blue blood politicians as well.

2. Social Clubs

Another way to meet a lot of rich men is to join an elite social club. There are usually fees involved but that's a small price to pay. If you can't afford a membership, try to befriend someone who is a member and attend events with them. Or if available, buy tickets to specific events hosted by the club. Yacht Clubs and Country Clubs are two types of social clubs were men of means congregate.

3. Hotels

Luxury hotels exist in every major city. You may not be able to afford a room at one of these establishments, but certainly you can put down a few coins on a delectable 4/5 Star dinner, appetizer or if nothing else, a cocktail. Hotel restaurants and bars are where the visiting and local elite meet, greet and congregate. Placing yourself in the midst of these movers and shakers puts you in prime position to date rich men.

4. Classic Car Shows

I recently passed a classic car show that was taking place in a ritzy suburb of Chicago. I was on my way somewhere else so I couldn't stop but as I drove past the outdoor event, I took note of the cars on display and most importantly the men proudly standing beside their expensive toys. The cars on display were classic vehicles in superb condition. The men at their sides looked just as well maintained. Money was definitely on the scene. I made a mental note to pass this information along. *There you have it!*

5. Political Fundraisers

Political fundraisers bring out the big bucks. I'm not talking about the $50/plate dinners held for the general public, I'm talking about the $1,000+ a plate fundraisers that attract people with incomes over $100,000/year. These events are set up beautifully for networking and socializing. Not to mention, you most certainly will meet the honored candidate. I met Barack Obama this way.

It is at these fundraisers that single women can meet and mingle with wealthy, single men. I know you don't have a spare $1,000 to spend on a dinner that _might_ net you a man so here's a tip! Become a political volunteer.

Donate a few weekends of your time to the campaign of a politician in your city/town. Make sure you get to know the people who are in charge of volunteers and organizing events. And more importantly, make sure they know you. When big events and fundraisers you could never afford to attend on your own come up, offer to work the event. The day of the event, make sure you circulate, meeting people and mingling with the VIP attendees. I know a few political volunteers who were flown across the country for major events and who attended big money fundraisers just because they proved to be committed volunteers. These middle-class folks mingled with some of the biggest players in politics and some of the wealthiest political contributors in the U.S.

PEEP GAME!

These are just a few of the places you can REACH OUT and TOUCH wealthy men. Certainly there are others, but I'll have to put that information in a future publication. For now, start with the 5 hot spots listed above. You can thank me later!

Step 5
LEARN HOW THE GAME IS PLAYED

Anybody can meet a rich guy one time, but a small number of women manage to date wealthy men regularly and successfully. Even fewer manage to get these BIG FISH to the altar.

I want you to win. I want you to succeed at dating rich because that is what you desire. I want you to master attracting and developing meaningful (or at least beneficial) relationships with wealthy men because that's what you've employed me to do.

In order to do that, I need to teach you THE GAME. I need to give you the inside track on dating rich so that you can eventually (if you choose) marry well.

The tips I shared above will certainly get you some face time with a few *Rich Cats*, but the following tips will surely take those connections as far as you want them to go.

PEEP GAME!

RULE #1

-WHATEVER YOU INTRODUCE, YOU MUST CONTINUE TO PRODUCE-

Whatever role you present to your wealthy man day one, is the role you must play throughout the relationship. If you present a sassy personality day one, don't become mousy 3 months into the relationship. If you present yourself as a flirtatious, self-confident tease day one, don't all of a sudden become shy and insecure about your looks. If you present yourself with glamorous/high-fashion style day one, don't start showing up to dates in grunge gear a month later.

Whatever you present date one is what your new beau will expect to see months down the line. Nobody likes a bait and switch situation so keep your PRESENTATION within reach of the real you. It is okay to change a little as your new relationship matures (THAT'S CALLED 'RUNNING GAME'), but doing a 180 degree switcheroo is no Bueno.

Meet the expectation! Remember, you set that bar day one.

RULE #2

-GET IN WHERE YOU FIT IN-

Whatever relationship you sign up for (casual dating, pay for play, arm candy/trophy girlfriend, etc.) is the relationship you agreed to. Know your position in the equation AND PLAY THAT POSITION! That's one major rule of the game. Don't agree to one thing and then try to Segway into something else later on!

Agree only to arrangements you can emotionally handle.

For instance, don't act like you're just looking for a sugar daddy when you really want a serious relationship that will lead to marriage. Don't present a cash for ass mentality if you really don't want to be a booty call. Don't act like you're okay being a mistress if you can't handle being a mistress.

Remember, a wealthy guy is like a beautiful woman…he has options. You don't want to lose a good catch playing silly games. Play the role you accepted when the two of you met and operate within that position.

Furthermore, decide ahead of time, what kind of dating relationship you want. Casual? Casual Sex? Sugar Daddy? Long-Term Relationship?

When you meet your rich man, communicate WHAT YOU REALLY WANT!

The opportunity to redefine the relationship and your role within that relationship may appear down the line, so if you fell into something you don't like, you may be able to change it later. **(Example: You two start out as friends with benefits but after dating a while you decide you want to be this guy's main chick)** You will know when that time comes because the two of you have unconsciously slipped into the desired relationship. You talk every night. (I.E. You make time for one another. You spend time together outside the bedroom, etc.)

Unless or until that happens however, play it safe. Stick to the original game plan.

RULE #3

-WHEN YOU CHOOSE THE MAN, YOU CHOOSE HIS LIFESTYLE-

Do you want a rich man? Do you really? Even if he works 24/7 and has very little time to dedicate to you? Do you want a man who travels days at a time? Do you want a man who women constantly pursue?

When you choose the experience you choose the circumstances that compliment that experience. We all WANT IT ALL but in reality, we can't have it all.

Rich men have a lot of money but often have very little personal time. Their focus is career and/or money…not necessarily cuddling with a woman every night. They also tend to travel a lot.

They may have a lot of social obligations and are often in the company of other women (secretaries, assistants, subordinates, etc.) Can you handle that?

If you want to be with a rich man, you are going to have to embrace **his** lifestyle. After all, he's the one with the leverage (financially speaking) in your relationship.

Let's take a look at the reality of dating a rich man:

- **He may not be home for dinner.**
- **He may work until 9 pm and leave at 7 am the next morning.**
- **He may travel with a female assistant.**
- **He may have to entertain female clients.**
- **He may not cook or help a lot with the kids.**

If you're used to dating the 9-5 guy, the rich man's lifestyle may seem like too much to handle. The reality is, every choice comes with a set of circumstances.

The lux life comes with a number of challenges and not every woman can handle those challenges…and (I must say)…there are nice middle and lower income men for those women!

But you? You CAN adjust. You can rise to the challenge. You can ADAPT and THRIVE in a rich relationship.

You can do this girl! All you have to do is open yourself to it. Expand your mind. There's nothing to it but to do it!

RULE # 4

-ASK! THAT'S THE ONLY WAY YOU'LL RECEIVE-

The media will insist rich guys hate women who want their money. The reality is, rich men are used to footing the bill and don't mind paying for the company they keep. I've never met a man who refused to buy me a drink, dinner, clothing, etc…who could afford that drink, dinner, clothing, etc.

PEEP GAME PLAYA! MEN WITH MONEY DON'T MIND SPENDING MONEY!

Take a minute and re-read the quote above from rapper 50 Cent. Go on. I'll wait.

As 50's quote insists…wealthy men know a financially conscious woman has certain expectations and in most cases, they are more than willing to meet those expectations.

They know how the game is played!

That said, you too must learn and respect the game. *Ask for what you want!* Remember, a closed mouth won't get fed. Ask your rich man for the material things you want believing you will receive!

As I explained, men with money don't mind spending it. If you can grab a guy's attention and narrow his focus to you…you can ask him for the things you desire and ultimately receive them. That's *Female Player 101*!

RULE # 5

-PREPARE TO GO THE DISTANCE-

If you are like most women today, you will be in the dating game for at least 10 years. And it's not totally unrealistic to assume you may be a single and available girl for 20 years.

➡ 16 yrs. old + 20 yrs. in the dating pool = 36 yrs. old

That presents a unique challenge. That challenge is, dating around without giving the appearance you have 'been around'.

What many ambitious women do when they are looking for a specific kind of guy is…run through men. They date and date and date believing quantity will get them to the JACKPOT GUY faster than being selective.

Today it's Joe. Tomorrow it's Ken. Next week it's John. Next month it's Sam.

I have seen many PlayGirls fall short of their relationship goals because they spread themselves too thin. Believe it or not, if you date voraciously, within a few years' time you have dated most of the eligible bachelors in your extended social circle. Your network is depleted because you've either dated a guy or dated his brother or dated his cousin or dated his friend.

If you don't want to be that girl, you will need to be creative with your dating practices. I can write a book on just that subject but for the purpose of this "Date Rich" book remember one thing: DON'T SPREAD YOURSELF TOO THIN.

- **Pick your Targets carefully**
- **Feel them out quickly**
- **If it's not a fit, get rid of him before things get sexual or too emotional**

One of the things I teach my clients is this:

A Female Player Dates Strategically!

Her moves are thought out. She plays THE DATING GAME rather than getting PLAYED by the GAME. Strategy is everything! Believe that.

You see, dating is like weight management. You cannot have everything offered to you. You must be selective in your choices.

It may be tempting to date friends, brothers or even fathers and sons, but the reality is, your reputation will suffer in the long run. And in the DATING GAME, reputation is everything!

READ MORE ON REPUTATION IN MY BOOK "HOW TO BE A FEMALE PLAYER: THE FUNDAMENTALS"

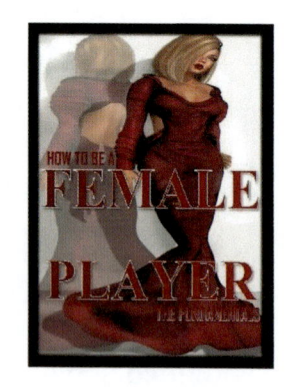

Remember, perception is reality! People believe what they SEE. You may not be a saint, but you can always give the illusion that you are. In THE DATING GAME, you must always avoid the appearance of impropriety.

Trust me on this. There are 2 things that devalue a woman's stock. One of them is dating too many men in the same dating pool.

Step 6
FINAL TIPS

Now, I've schooled you on how to attract rich men and I've told you how to get your foot in that door with the wealthy and elite. If you follow my advice to the letter, you should have no problem meeting men who have money and getting what you want from them.

Before I end this lesson I want to share a few final tips with you…that will surely take your *Date Rich, Marry Well Game* to the next level.

1. KNOW YOUR STRENGTHS AND WEAKNESSES:

One of the Fundamentals of Mackin' (men) that I teach my clients is just that. You have to know what you are working with and what you have working against you IF you want to capitalize off of your gifts and play down your weaknesses.

Are you attractive? Do you have a beautiful body? Are you a good conversationalist? These are STRENGHTHS. Capitalize off of whatever you have working for you even if the only thing you have going for you is great fashion sense.

Are you shy in groups? Do you lack personality? Do you talk too much? Are you unattractive? Tough questions, but if you want to master the dating game, you are going to have to look at yourself impersonally.

Know thyself! Play UP your strengths so that they MASK your weaknesses.

2. DEVELOP A HOOK THAT WORKS FOR YOU:

A hook is your script or line that you use to get what you want from men. Your hook will be different from my hook and my hook will be different from the next woman's.

For some women (who date men with money), their hook is need related. They will present a need and ask the money man to meet that demand. Single mothers and college students often use that hook.

For other women the hook is a tease—a promise of sorts. She implies the relationship will go to a higher level IF the rich guy pleases her. Sex may be implied. In other cases, the impression is given that a long-term relationship is imminent. This is a go to hook for many single women who are not really looking for a husband.

Again, the hook is your script. It's a line you throw out for the Target to catch. Every player uses a hook. Decide on and perfect yours.

3. SEDUCTION WILL NET YOU MORE THAN SEX:

Don't strive to sex men down as a way of 'securing' them. Rather, work on your Target's mind with a powerful seduction. Sex is but a moment of pleasure. Seduction (if done properly) so impacts the mind and emotions that the Target is wrapped up in its spell for weeks, months, even years.

The woman who can get a man to think irrationally, can have all that she pleases.

There you have it! That is THE GAME on dating rich and marrying well.

I look forward to your success. With the knowledge I just gave you, you cannot lose. Be well PlayGirl! And as you rise UP, remember who put you up on G.A.M.E....

I AM THE FEMALE MACK

Butta 'Fly' Jonez

OTHER BOOKS BY BUTTA 'FLY' JONEZ

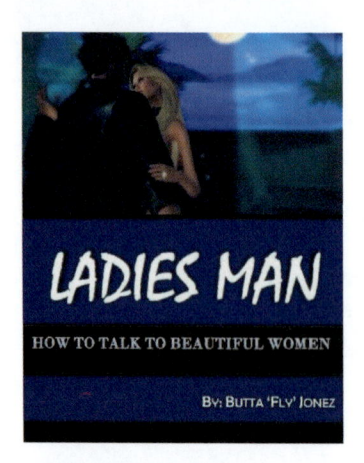

LADIES MAN
HOW TO TALK TO BEAUTIFUL WOMEN
By: Butta 'Fly' Jonez

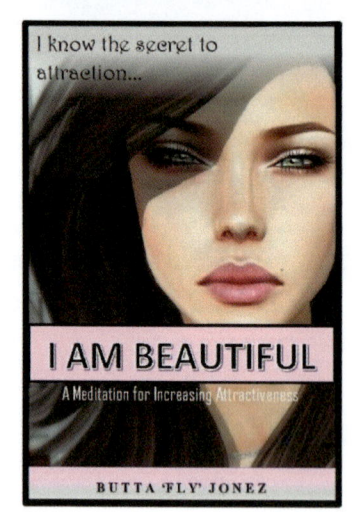

I AM BEAUTIFUL
I know the secret to attraction...
A Meditation for Increasing Attractiveness
BUTTA 'FLY' JONEZ

AVAILABLE NOW VIA

AMAZON.COM

AND

BUTTAJONEZ.COM

ABOUT BUTTA 'FLY' JONEZ

Butta 'Fly' Jonez is a dating game expert. She is known world-wide as The Female Mack, a testament to her unusual ability to game and tame men. Jonez founded "The Playa's Guide" (PeepGame.Net) in 2010, which garnered her worldwide recognition. Fans enjoyed the daily commentary but kept asking ButtaFly to detail her knowledge in a book.

"How to be a Female Player: The Fundamentals" was released in December 2013. "Date Rich, Marry Well" is the highly-anticipated follow-up to that groundbreaking book.

Through Butta 'Fly' Jonez' #HOWTOBEAFEMALEPLAYER book series, women all over the world are learning how to date strategically and effectively like a female player. Men too, are now learning THE GAME from Butta Jonez through her new line of books called, "Ladies' Man".

"Don't hate the players" Jonez is famous for saying, "just learn how to play the game."

JOIN ME ON SOCIAL MEDIA!

Twitter:

@ButtaJonez

Facebook:

@ButtaJonezTheFemaleMack

READ MY NEW ADVICE COLUMN "CONFESSIONS OF A FEMALE MACK" AT BUTTAJONEZ.COM.

Printed in Great Britain
by Amazon.co.uk, Ltd.,
Marston Gate.